10 SIGNS of a
CHEATER-TO-BE

by

DR. GILDA CARLE

Published in New York by
InterChange Communications Training, Inc.

ISBN-13: 978-1-881829-14-0

Library of Congress Control Number: 2015904358

Printed in the United States

For more information visit
www.DrGilda.com

ACKNOWLEDGMENTS

Thank you to all who have so generously contributed your true stories to help others who are reading this book. Without your giving, there would be less healthful living!
--Dr. Gilda

<u>Gilda-Gram®</u>
Learn your honey's history,
and you'll be able to predict your future.

CONTENTS

INTRODUCTION

The Signs of a Cheater-to-Be Are Evident

Gilda-Gram®
**THE SIGNS of a cheater-to-be are evident—
if only the needy-for-love would read them!**

Most of us —even the not-so-jealous types— know that awful feeling: "Is my love really working late… or could s/he be two-timing me?" I've counseled lots of folks, Single, married, and somewhat in between, who deal with this concern more than they need to. Wondering whether you're being cheated on can bring all encompassing pain. Here are my findings about the most common SIGNS that your honey is cheating, or at least, seriously contemplating it.

Use this information and insight—and either stop worrying, or have a serious heart-to-heart with yourself, and then with your partner! The objective is to let go of pain that will bring you down personally, and eventually derail your relationship as it eats away at your feelings of self-esteem and happiness. In the end, don't you want to enjoy a healthy relationship truly built on trust?

10 SIGNS
of a Cheater-to-Be

SIGN #1
Your Honey Keeps You a Secret

Cheaters keep you in the dark while they play in the light. Your relationship won't work if you're getting what I call the Shadow Treatment.

Sometime actress, merchandise empress, and former queen of MySpace, Tila (Tequila) Nguyen, was named by Time magazine "the least lonely girl on the Internet" with 1.5 million "friends" on her web site. She said she had a three-year liaison with actor Jared Leto, one-time fiancé of Cameron Diaz. She described him as "sweet to me when nobody is around, but when we are around other people, he acts like a different person." Despite her popularity on the web, as well as her other achievements, the Vietnamese beauty said Leto kept their affair hidden. She herself allowed the deception by continuing to describe on MySpace an affair she was having with "an actor," without ever naming him. Leto's Shadow Treatment made sense—at least to him— because during that time, he had also been linked to Lindsay Lohan and Scarlett Johansson.

Dear Dr Gilda
My boyfriend of 11 months has been living with
his ex-wife for the last 14 years. Although they have no
children, he says it is just for convenience. He is well
off, and he can afford to move out on his own. He
professes to love me more than life itself, and has
promised to tell his family about me.

His family does not visit him at his ex-wife's
place, so he instead visits them every week. Yet, he has
never mentioned me to them. He asked me to give him
time, but nothing has changed. Now he wants one more
month. He insists that I am the most important person in
his life. What should I do?
Do I Have the Plague?

Dear Do I Have the Plague?,
Your well-off guy is in a very comfy emotional
position with his ex-wife. Is this a sexually expedient
convenience? Are they best platonic friends? Does he
depend on her for emotional support during times of
need? Does she depend on him for emotions or
finances? In other words, exactly what kind of
relationship are they in? Fourteen years is a very long
time, and they obviously have a deep bond that you
inevitably would have to cut into.

When we first start seeing someone, of course,
that person's living arrangements should not be our
concern. But you and this guy have been together for
almost a year now. Not only don't you fully understand
what goes on between him and his "domestic partner,"
you also don't have a clue as to why he insists on
keeping you a secret from his family. Is there some

connection between his family and the relationship he has with his ex?

As an outsider looking in, this is certainly a mystery to me, but I'm not the one who must be impressed with Boyfriend's honesty; YOU are!

There are two separate—or connected—issues here: Dude's living arrangements for the past 14 years, and his refusal to let his family know about you. Those are the relationship aspects.

But also, there is a third issue, too, in that you have allowed Boyfriend's evasive behavior to plague, yes, plague, the feelings you have regarding yourself. No, girl, you don't have "the plague," but your choice in men very well may!

Before you move forward, find out what has truly evolved over the past fourteen years to keep Boyfriend living with his ex. Observe his behavior for signs of dependency, a need to be needed, and his feelings about sexual convenience.

When you have gathered the truth about this, and you are satisfied with what you find, then discover WHY he has kept you at arm's length from his relatives. As I say, this may be a separate issue, or one that is connected to the former.

In any case, you can't possibly have a lasting relationship with someone who keeps you as a shadow. Before you commit yourself to Mystery Man, be sure the guy has completely removed his mask.

Otherwise, he's cheating you out of his emotional presence!
Dr. Gilda

Nancy had been seeing a man for five years, but he hid her from his ex from whom he had been divorced for 15 years! He and his ex didn't have children together, so he couldn't even use that as his excuse for wanting to remain close to her. While he continued to bend over backwards to please this ex, he continued to tell Nancy he loved her, and that she was the only woman he wanted in his life. So she, in turn, hung in there.

But over the years, for family gatherings, Nancy was excluded if his ex was expected to be in attendance. He told Nancy that at one time his ex discovered that he had fallen in love again—and she was devastated. He said he didn't want to cause such pain for her again. He further said that if Nancy made him choose between his ex and her, she would lose.

This guy was cheating Nancy out of his attention—whether he was actually physically cheating with his ex or not.

<u>Gilda-Gram®</u>
"Cheating" doesn't exclusively mean
inserting Flap A into Slot B.

Cheating can also suggest a diverting of attention away from the person purported to be "the one" to someone entirely different. The person who is in the shadows is constantly left feeling like an outsider in the relationship.

People who get the Shadow Treatment are often kept waiting in the wings while their mate is having a grand old time socializing elsewhere. Think about it: Are there gatherings of friends, family reunions or workplace parties you are not invited to? Do you only meet some of your honey's friends and family?

Margie had been seeing Ray for five years. They lived a long drive of two hours away from each other. They were both in their late 30's, and he had a ten-year-old child from a previous marriage whom he saw on alternate weekends. As close as the couple seemed to be, Margie had never met this child. Ray kept promising it would happen, but on each occasion, there was some excuse that prevented it. And each excuse was plausible: Ray's father had just died, and the child was mourning his grandfather; the boy had major baseball practice for an upcoming championship game; the child had contracted a bad case of the flu. Over the course of five years, even the "plausible" excuses were wearing thin. Still, Margie held on.

Ray said he was saving money to buy her an engagement ring, and that he'd like to tie the knot sometime in the year that followed. But he was making a lot of money as a stockbroker, and the excuse of not having enough money saved seemed shallow. However,

Margie wanted to get married so badly, she accepted the excuses along with the rest of their relationship as it was.

After all this time, as a result of Margie's urging, Ray finally orchestrated a meeting between his girlfriend and his mother. The pair went out for a two-hour lunch. During their time together, the mom peculiarly went on and on about how poor a marriage partner Ray would make. Her rationale was that he had been married before, and as soon as he tied the knot, he became emotionally distant and cold to his wife.

What a lunch that had been! Instead of feeling welcomed into the family, Margie left perplexed about why a mother would bother to meet her, and then rat out her own son. Margie considered that maybe Ray's mom just didn't like her. If Margie ever felt unsure of this romance, she now also questioned her self-worth.

When she returned to Ray with details of her experience with his mother, he told her to ignore his mom's behavior. He said she had not taken his divorce well, especially since she felt she had lost her closeness with her grandson as a result of it. Ray never confronted his mom about the way she treated Margie, and Margie was expected to take this all in stride. Margie still had not met Ray's son.

Finally, the time had arrived when Ray said he had wanted to present her with an engagement ring. This time, when push finally came to shove, he said he was no longer sure about their future. Moreover, she "accidentally" discovered that there was another woman hanging around Ray, with whom he often had dinner.

While Margie could detect no guarantee that she and Ray were an item, it certainly seemed suspicious. This was the first time in 5 years that Margie questioned her man's fidelity.

Margie felt as though she had suddenly been hit in the stomach. She questioned her sanity about being with a man for five long years who made empty promises he never thought he'd keep. Why did she allow herself to be given the Shadow Treatment for so long? Clearly, she needed to examine her own desperation for love, and how she had been allowing it to blind her from the reality of what she was getting back from the man who allegedly loved her.

If you are kept on the sidelines, there's usually a good reason. Maybe your sweetie is on the prowl for someone else. Or perhaps there already IS someone else, and that's why your role in his/her life can't be made public. Anytime you are kept on the fringes when you think you are an exclusive couple, beware. The only way to end Shadow Treatment is to stop accepting it. Once you challenge the way things are, you will either be fully welcomed in your sweetheart's life... or you will know it's time to leave.

In short, the only way to end Shadow Treatment is to stop accepting it.

Gilda-Gram®
If your sweetie doesn't think you're worth being acknowledged, your sweetie's not worth being in your life!

SIGN #2
Your Honey Is Emotionally or Physically Absent

Cheaters often conceal their *emotional* whereabouts so they can be evasive about their *physical* whereabouts. And sometimes they conceal their *physical* whereabouts to be evasive about their *emotional* whereabouts. In whichever way it may play out, love will be exhausting when you must pry the truth out of a partner who, to your face, swears that you're "the one," but shows you otherwise through his or her disrespectful behavior.

Dear Dr Gilda,

I am in a relationship with a man I used to date when he was single. After a few months of our dating, he returned to his ex girlfriend, but we still kept on seeing each other. Finally, I told him I didn't want to do this anymore, and I stopped seeing him for good.

But a year later, he came back into my life, and we started dating again. He was very single. After a few months, we exchanged words of love, and I met his friends. I found out that he was having an affair as a threesome with his best friend and his wife for six years! And they are now in my life with my boyfriend, as well as being my friends. That means that the whole time he was with his ex and me, he was also having sex with his friends!!

When I asked about this, he lied about how long he had been doing this, and when he stopped. He said he loves me, and wants only me. But I don't trust him.

I do love him, and I'm happy with him. I can't sleep, and I get upset and sick when I see his friend's wife. How can I move past this? Should I stay with him and forgive him?
Upset and Confused

Dear Upset and Confused,
Okay, so you now know that Boyfriend is a liar and a cheater. Yet, you say, "I do love him, and I'm happy with him." So let me ask you this: What do you love about this dude? Sure, he said he "loves" you, and "wants only" you. Can you believe these words? As the saying goes, "Talk is cheap." Boyfriend has been lying to you for a long time. This was disrespectful to you and to what you thought you had with him. Now, you're rewarding his lies and behavior by returning to his bedroom, and hoping for a life with him!

While you want to know whether you can "move past this," I wonder if Boyfriend has moved past his longstanding desire for threesomes, and his lying about it. Everyone's behavior is rooted in some historical significance to that person. For example, did Boyfriend grow up in a home where he had to jockey for power? Did he feel he was in competition with another male figure, maybe even his father, for his mother's love? What is the meaning to him of having multiple partners in bed together at the same time?

While you think you may know Boyfriend well enough to "love" him, until you understand him and are fully aware of why he practices—or practiced—this sort of sexual activity, you don't even have a clue about what makes him tick. Unless you know someone really well, you are just setting yourself up for pain.

Of course, I'm focusing just on Boyfriend's sexual predilections. But you're part of this alleged love equation. So ask yourself why you insist on returning to this guy after you know the truth.

Of course you don't trust him at this point. How could you? But to think you will wave a magic wand and change him is a misconception of a lot of couples starting out. In the end, their hopes and dreams are doomed.

I'm sorry that this feedback is not more hopeful, but it would be foolish to jump into a lifelong wish, only to find that you duped yourself into believing you had something that was not there.
Dr. Gilda

Yes, we often dupe ourselves into thinking that a leopard's spots will miraculously change once our status with that leopard does. Whether a couple has officially merged together or not, a major Sign of a fruitful future relationship is a foundation of honesty.

After enjoying a platonic friendship for a decade, Carol and Ben began seriously dating over the course of two years. Ben was a traveling sales manager. While he was on the road, Carol heard from him only occasionally, but that's when they would spend hours on the phone long into the night, talking long distance. While Carol would have preferred a more constant presence from Ben, she was seduced by the times that he did call and have these intense conversations with her. She rationalized that this is just the way he is. And so she continued to hang on.

Ben continued to tell this woman he wanted to spend more time with her, which gave Carol hope for a future together. But that extra time to be spent together never came to pass. The excuses were always blamed on Ben's travel demands, which any woman in love certainly understood.

Carol's friend tried to talk sense into her, pointing out that she was obviously a low priority for Ben. But Carol refused to see this. She insisted on taking Ben at his word, ignoring the Signs that clearly pointed to the fact that she was merely a convenience for this man.

One day, she and Ben had just arrived at his apartment after spending a glorious day at the park with his dog. They were both seemingly happy and exhilarated. He innocently played back a voice mail left on his blinking answering machine. It was from a woman who obviously knew him very, very, VERY well. She detailed how their most recent lovemaking, out of all the times they had been together previously, was explosive, and she was looking forward to a repeat performance the next time he was in her town.

Carol's jaw dropped, as Ben sheepishly tried to explain that what she heard was not what it seemed to be. *Oh, sure! Then what could it have been?* Carol was not only shocked to learn Ben had another girlfriend across the country, but she also felt like a jerk for having allowed Ben's physical and emotional absences to go unquestioned. She walked out of Ben's place, and refused to take any of his calls after that. Ten years as great friends went down the tubes, along with the two years she and Ben had been a "committed" couple—or so she thought. Carol felt the great loss, but she realized that it would have been even greater had she gotten any closer to this cheater.

Emotionally and physically absent partners may say what you want to hear, but they will not change their actions—unless they want to. And nobody *wants* to change his/her ways unless s/he feels the need to on his/her own. At the point this couple was at, there was never a need for Ben to alter his actions because, until he was caught, he was having the time of his life!

Saying the right thing and doing the right thing are very different. An emotionally and/or physically absent partner is just that: ABSENT. If your honey talks a good game about spending more time with you, but never delivers—look out! This person may be juggling multiple relationships, semi-commitments, and loads of promises to untold numbers of people. As the saying goes, talk is cheap. In the end, the only thing of any consequence is the way you are treated.

<u>Gilda-Gram®</u>
**Words may camouflage what a cheater is doing,
but behavior tells the truth.**

<u>SIGN #3</u>
Your Honey Wants a
No-Strings-Attached Romance

If someone declares, "I don't want a commitment," take the sucker at his or her word! Don't ask questions, or try to reason with this declaration. That's how this person feels—and that's what you must respect. End of story.

After two years of loneliness, Tim met Clara on the Internet. She told him upfront, "I'm married, so don't expect anything." He said he respected her honesty, and actually found it "refreshing." *Come on, dude, how "honest" is Clara if she's willing to "play" with you, even though she's married??*

First they emailed occasionally, and then they emailed each other every day. Eventually, they upped the ante to the phone. Finally, they met—and ended up in bed. Clara revealed her unhappiness in her twelve-year marriage, which Tim suspected all along, since she was devoting a lot of time communicating with him, rather than with her husband.

Tim persuaded her to leave her husband, and move in with him. She agreed to do just that. But only five days after the move, she announced, "I need space. I got out of one marriage, and now I feel I'm in another."

Totally brokenhearted and emotionally destroyed, that was the last time Tim saw Clara. *Duh! Did he really expect more??*

Don't ever fall into the "I'll-be-the-one-to-change-all-that!" trap. Most adults rebel against someone wanting to control them, but cheaters, in particular, resent anyone getting *thisclose* that their antics might be revealed for what they truly are. If a cheater is especially put upon, he or she may even have an affair just to spite a partner who wants to rein him or her in.

Too often, people block out the clear message a potential date has sent. The person wearing a marriage band trumpets, "I'm not going to be available for you." But some people pursue marrieds just the same—hoping they can pry him or her away from an allegedly comfy nest. Let that notion go!

It's unusual for married people to permanently leave home for someone with whom they are just, in their mind, playing. In fact, one person who did break up her marriage to be with her also-married lover, confessed after ten years with him, "If I had known then what I know now, I would have stayed put with my very loving ex-husband, who, at the time, I (mis)perceived as being 'boring.'" WOW!!

If someone clearly mutters these telling phrases: "I'm not into serious relationships," or "I love my freedom," or "I'm not ready to settle down," hear those words for what they are—and take a giant step back! The person is clearly defining his or her modus

DR. GILDA CARLE

operandi, which is, "I enjoy my current status, and I want to continue playing the field—and, perhaps, sleeping with you while I do."

Sure, a person might seduce you with lovely words or expensive gifts. But words and gifts send mixed messages, because:

Gilda-Gram®
Seducers aim to lube the tubes of sexual success.

If you choose to believe what you want to believe, and you decide to fall for a seducer anyway, you will probably find yourself disappointed and broken-hearted—if, that is, you want more. Of course, it depends on what you're after.

What you don't want is to try to manipulate someone into a situation he or she has already said s/he doesn't want to be in. If your honey tells you he or she doesn't want more than what you already have, accept that at face value, and if that's not okay with you, instead of trying to rationalize to make it okay, or to manipulate your lover to change his or her mind, *move on*!

Tony continued to tell Marylou he loved her. Whenever he visited her, he brought flowers and little thoughtful gifts that proved he cared. After six very romantic months, when Marylou finally asked, "Tony, darling, where are we going with this?" he said he didn't feel their "souls" would interact well down the road, and

16

where they were at this point in time was as far as he wanted their affair to go. *Whaaaaat?*

Marylou was dumbfounded. The couple shared many things in common, they spoke the same language of peace in the world, they were both Yoga instructors dedicated to their art, and their friends literally "felt" the chemistry they emitted. Yet, Tony was reluctant to take the plunge into a life-long commitment—at least with her.

Yes, despite what Tony told her, naïve Marylou allowed the relationship to continue for six more months, hoping he'd eventually come around. They lived in the same small town, so they saw each other day and night. When an appliance broke in Marylou's apartment, Tony ran over to fix it. When she went to teach a course in Paris, Tony watched over everything for her, and called her every day with a progress report. To any outsider looking in, it was obvious he cared deeply for Marylou. But something was holding him back.

One day, Marylou was driving past his house, hurriedly trying to get to an appointment for which she was very late. But she was not too late to miss Tony emerging from his home with a beautiful blonde on his arm. Marylou brought her brakes to a screeching halt. She sat there and stared. Tony saw her, and was speechless. So that was what the poppycock regarding their "souls" not interacting was all about! Marylou vowed never to see Tony again.

You can't push people beyond their comfort

zone. Listen to what they say, listen to what they omit, and observe every bit of their body language. This way, you'll surely be able to detect the clues that reveal the score! But once you know what that score is, ACCEPT IT AND BE ON YOUR WAY!!

<u>Gilda-Gram®</u>
People "tell" you what they want
through their words and behavior.
Hear them!

SIGN #4
Your Honey Admits to Cheating on Exes—and Justifies It

Cheaters rationalize their behavior to let themselves off the hook. But the way they justify their actions tells much about their character.

Listen to the excuses for past cheating your sweetie uses. Here are several I've collected over the years from some clients:

- "Although I do love Roger, I don't feel the passion for him that I feel for Jay."

- "Although Peter might be my husband, I'm happiest when I'm with Joe. You *do* want me to be happy, Dr. Gilda, don't you?"

- "My wife is very ill. We socialize with a couple. The husband hates sex, but wants his wife to be satisfied. So she and I have gotten together with his encouragement. My wife doesn't know, but since she's so sick, I don't think it matters."

- "I have loved the same man for 36 years, but I married to someone else. My husband is good to me now, but he used to be abusive because of a drinking problem. Now I want to be with my lover full time. I have teenage children and I'm afraid."

- "I was a sexually abused child, and my father cheated on my mom. Cheating on my girlfriend now is my way of getting back at,   equalizing, and controlling my past."

It sure seems that everyone has a tale to tell, and the more practiced a person is with his or her story, the more convincing it might sound to you. If you're hearing rationalizations from your honey, ask yourself whether they are *really* acceptable to you?

A person who admits to infidelities in the past, and explains them away with calm and candor, will probably stray again without apology. This person is not taking responsibility for his or her past actions, nor has he or she worked through the issues that were originally at the heart of this behavior.

So in the end, as far as you're concerned, hanging out with this person after you know the truth will then become YOUR issue.

Further, if you accept your honey's indiscretions and explanations, you're unwittingly teaching him or her that this behavior is okay with you. *Is it really??*

Gilda-Gram®
What we accept, we teach.

Just wait until Honey begins to rationalize to someone else the reasons he or she strayed on you! Then how okay will it be?

SIGN #5
Your Honey Has Never Been without a Mate

Cheaters won't ride solo . . . ever! Leaving one romance and hopping into a new one—or having simultaneous affairs at once—doesn't leave time for assessing whatever went wrong in the past. Cheaters don't bother with introspection; their focus is squarely set on pulling new people into their orbit. If you are dating a person who shares a romantic history that always involves finding a new partner before or while breaking up with the current partner, take heed. This person may think of you only as a void-filler. Filling a void is never a basis for lasting love.

Kate was married 2½ times. Why the ½? Officially, she had two bona fide ex-husbands, and she was now engaged to the man who was to be Husband #3. He was a great guy, good-natured, and only too happy to give Kate everything she wanted. What a change from her former husband who was cheap and nasty to her.

Unfortunately, Kate had a bottomless pit of desire for everything. Husband-to-Be #3 bought her diamonds, furs, a new house with an elevator that they would soon move into, and a big Jaguar, the car she had always dreamed of having. But Kate was never happy because no one could fill her true feelings of inadequacy. What she felt for this man wasn't love at all, but a need-fulfillment.

On the sly, she began to see her second husband with whom she had had a turbulent and very angry "War of the Roses" divorce. She was convinced that her second husband was truly the man for her, although they could not get along at all. When Husband-to-Be #3 discovered Kate's affair, he was shocked and heartbroken. He said he knew that Kate always re-coupled quickly. And now he also recognized that meeting her when her divorce was still ongoing had been a big mistake.

Kate went on to break it off with Husband-to-Be #3, and actually re-marry her second husband. At this point, to get her to re-commit, the nasty cheapskate promised to give her a large sum of money at the time of their nuptials.

As soon as they tied the knot, however, the man reneged on his promise to give her massive riches, and Kate now felt caged in a marriage that should never have occurred even the first time.

Jeff and Sara had been together exclusively for six years. She took a dream job out of state, while Jeff stayed behind to complete an internship for his job. When they reunited, neither was particularly excited to see the other. But neither was willing to discuss their feelings about what was truly going on in their hearts.

After Sara returned to her new home, Jeff began

cheating on her with Sally. He rationalized, "I am getting older, and I only want to be with Sally if I know for sure it would be long-term. Otherwise, I will stay with Sara because of how much I've already invested in that relationship."

For Jeff, women were merely void-fillers. Filling a void may fill some empty feelings, but it can never offer the foundation for a lasting love.

If your honey seems incapable of being alone, you don't need a magnifying glass to perceive his or her neediness. Neediness and desperation eventually derail even the best of relationships, because a needy and desperate mate is not with YOU for YOU, but to fill a need in him or her that is empty. Rest assured that even if you fill that empty space, your honey will still want for more, because emptiness can never be filled by another person. This is work that each person must do on his or her own.

Telling Question: Do you want to be someone's love, or do you want to be someone's filler? *No one's looking; be true to yourself when you respond to this.*

Telling Answer: Your honest response to this Telling Question will determine your love future!

Gilda-Gram®
Lonely people seek hobbies.
Insecure people seek lovers.

SIGN #6
Your Honey Lies about Little Things

Cheaters lie even about things that seem silly and inconsequential. You are always left to question their truth from their fiction. As my Gilda-Gram says, "When the need to embroider overshadows the desire for honesty, the relationship is a sham."

Craig's friend set him up on a blind date with divorcée, Alice, who was a top attorney in their town with no children. Each time they were together, Alice described her interesting caseload. Craig was fascinated—and he was quickly falling hard. He was so caught up in her charismatic personality that he chose not to focus on the fact that some of her stories contradicted themselves, and that Alice seemed to change certain details each time she told a story twice.

By this time, the couple was seeing each other for four months. One day, the local newspaper featured someone who had been indicted for impersonating an attorney. Craig was just browsing the paper, when he gasped to find Alice's photo as the person who was indicted. Moreover, she was a wife and mother as well! Alice had lied to both Craig and their mutual friend who fixed them up.

If you are dating someone who seems to be untruthful even about mundane topics — where s/he had

lunch, what s/he is doing on Sunday morning, when s/he goes to the gym — take note. The little lies probably run a lot deeper than you can imagine.

Gilda-Gram®
Without truth, there can be no love.

Don't you believe you DESERVE more? If you're not truly sure, read my book, "I'm Worth Loving! Here's Why." It will surely open your eyes to what you truly DESERVE!!

Certainly, if you don't believe you DESERVE more than you're getting, you're more likely to accept cheating from a cheater. But once you recognize you have the right to know whom you invite into your bed, you'll be more assertive about asking appropriate questions regarding inappropriate behaviors.

Gilda-Gram®
Lies are uncovered when we question inconsistencies when they arise.

SIGN #7
Your Honey Brags about Having Great Sex Appeal

Cheaters are insecure, and they don't stop trying to attract constant attention. They flaunt their popularity in attempts to boost their own low self-esteem. Marilyn met a "hot guy" on a singles cruise, and the pair became inseparable for the week. When they returned home, they spoke to each other constantly. He sent her a plane ticket to visit him. While together, Hot Guy boasted that he was his town's "go-to" guy for all the lonely and sex-starved women. Instead of Marilyn reading that as a SIGN to stay away, she naively interpreted his description of himself as "oh so cute."

Visiting her two weeks later, he said he was available for her throughout the week—except for a lunch date he had with a woman he had just met. Marilyn found that peculiar, but said nothing. When they were together, after a dinner party he took her to, he detailed how many women had come on to him. Finally, Marilyn began feeling disrespected and put down. On his last night in town, and after crying herself to sleep the night before, she told Hot Guy he was too hot for her, as she bid him good-bye.

If a partner boasts how in demand s/he is, recognize how insecure s/he *really* is—and steer clear. Your honey probably needs more ego stroking than any one person can provide.

So now you know the signs that indicate that maybe your honey isn't such a honey after all. Life and love are all about learning—and sometimes that learning is painful.

Gilda-Gram®
Everyone who touches us, teaches us.

Instead of getting bummed out about a cheater who stole your heart, think of what you learned, and how your experience got you to grow. Your new insight will arm you to attract someone much more trustworthy in the future. And you'll be a lot happier.

Gilda-Gram®
Secure people know who they are,
and invite others to s-l-o-w-l-y find out.

SIGN #8
Your Honey's Family or Friends Cheat

Cheaters mirror what they saw while growing up, without even giving it a second thought. Children who observed cheating while they were developing, often apply this behavior to their own adult relationships, since that has always been their reality about how people in love act.

Through the years, Melanie observed how John would date women, cheat on them, and then dump them—just as his father did. They were friends, so it was inconsequential to Melanie how John treated women he dated. But then they evolved into a romance of their own.

Melanie never thought he'd treat her like any of the other women who came and went before her. She and John told each other how much love they felt, and agreed to be exclusive. But suddenly, seemingly out of nowhere, John announced that he was taking another woman out for Valentine's Day. Melanie admitted that that should have been her SIGN to lose this guy right then and there. But instead, she continued on and off with him for four torturous years.

It wasn't until after she caught him in his seventh

affair (!) that Melanie finally decided pulled the plug. *Some people take longer than others to see the light!!*

When she first met Todd, April was bowled over. He bought her expensive jewelry, flew her in his small plane, and impressed her to no end about all the famous people he worked with. April had been brought up in a lower middle class family, and everything she did in her life was a struggle. After her divorce, she singlehandedly raised three children when their father deserted them. So when Todd appeared with his apparent gravy train, how could she resist?

The couple quickly became inseparable. She gave up her meager job and began working with him as a producer of TV infomercials. Jobs would pay him in the five and six figures, and together they were reeling in the money. Because Todd was so busy producing, April began to take over the bookkeeping.

Soon, what she uncovered was not pretty. She found many hundreds of thousands of dollars in cash payments that Todd never reported to the IRS. When she mentioned this to her now husband, Todd brushed it off as "no big deal." They continued to travel extensively, stay in the finest hotels in the world, fly first class, and own expensive cars, boats, and other toys. What a life! She knew Todd cheated on her, but, at this point, who really cared? Her current life was a far cry from what April had been raised with, or what her deserting ex-husband had left her with.

But after ten years, the IRS caught up with Todd—and April, as his wife and business partner.

There was a trial, Todd went to jail, and although April was not charged in his elaborate business schemes, she was left penniless. Todd spent a few years behind bars, and then he was finally released.

Foolish April thought they'd resume their marriage as it was, and get back on the gravy train they had both enjoyed. But Todd had different ideas. He had already moved on to a woman thirty years April's junior. And most surprising to her, April couldn't believe how shabbily her husband was now treating her.

When she sought me out for counseling, I explained that people don't change—unless they are driven to turn a corner on their own. What was in it for Todd to want to change? His past life may have gotten him into legal trouble and put him in jail, but he reasoned that, for the most part, he had had a great run. And he was willing and anxious to resume the same thing again, to get his posh live back to where it had been. However, this time, he chose a new model as his partner in crime.

April was devastated. Not only did she not have any money now, but she was also in deep debt from the bills Todd had left her with, and for which she was also responsible as his wife. She felt used up and discarded. And now she felt old, when she considered his new lover. I asked her where she had been while he was stealing and laundering other people's money. She hadn't considered that:

Gilda-Gram®
**If he treats others badly, in time,
he'll treat US the same.**

Actually, April had never considered she might end up on Todd's hit list. She had been enjoying the rich life so much, she naively and probably selfishly disconnected herself from those innocent people that her husband was cheating.

Fortunately, after painful, but insightful, therapy, and a few more years of mourning, she re-connected with a former boyfriend who had always loved her. He was not flashy, she would have to live with much less, and she would need to return to living a bland, but very dependable life. In exchange for all that, she had a man who was honest and reliable, and someone she knew would never cheat others or her. When we last spoke, April was married, calmer, and so much happier.

Since we are products of our pasts, discover the history of your honey *during courtship*, before your heart has the misfortune of becoming trashed later.

Gilda-Gram®
**If a red flag waves, take note.
If a second appears, be on your guard.
If you see a third, BE ON YOUR WAY!**

SIGN #9
Your Honey is a Game Player

Cheaters think love is a game, and they enjoy enrolling unsuspecting partners in a play-off. But the words they use can quickly spill their secrets—IF you listen carefully.

Examine the words your honey uses. Do you hear game-playing language, such as "play it cool," "play hard to get," "play that person," or "manipulate to win"? For true game-players, the abiding goal of the love game is the chase, not the catch.

Do you think the following email to me would be classified as "game playing?"

Dear Dr. Gilda,

I have been married for 22 years. My wife has been going out to a club with two other women for eleven weeks straight, two to three nights a week, and she's never asked me to go until I mentioned it. We have a special needs child, so we don't get out alone much.

On the past two weekends, I met all the women at the club, and we had a good time. The last time, I told one of her friends that I wasn't planning on going. But I then changed my mind, and showed up. It wasn't a good night! At the end, I was going to dance with my wife, and I had my hand on her back. But she suddenly ran off to dance with a guy she knew.

On the way home, she called her friend to get that guy's phone number. When I confronted her the next day, she said it was stupid of her to do that. Her excuse was that she was drunk, and so was he. I don't think they even talked after she called him. She seems to have dialed the number, then hung up.

What is your opinion of her going clubbing so often with her girlfriends? And what is your opinion of her phone call to that guy?
Upset Husband

Dear Upset Husband,
The issue you describe is not the real issue you have! There's a problem with your marriage when your wife runs away from home each night, drops out of reality with alcohol and other men, and acts like an irresponsible teenager! Why are you not addressing this real issue?

Your wife is obviously quite miserable with life as it is. Is she very stressed with your special needs child? Is she angry with you because marriage hasn't been what she expected? When was the last time the two of you sat together, alcohol-free, and exchanged your thoughts, feelings, and goals for the future?

Your lady is harboring a lot of pent up emotion. What she needs is not a night out, or three, every week, but rather a safe environment to release this emotion. If she doesn't know how to provide it for herself, then you must.

A married mother getting drunk, slithering around a dance floor with strange men, and calling them for more, is setting the stage for blatant infidelity. I don't know whether this has already occurred, but the seeds are certainly being planted, under the guise of being "drunk."

Your life may be tough, but by not confronting the thorns in your marriage, you both choose to play the game of "stick-my-head-in-the-sand." The problem with this game is that there's only so much sand to cover you before you can no longer hide.

Why won't the two of you face the need to work on your marriage or call it quits? Yes, that's a scary notion. But the ramifications of your wife acting out as she is can eventually turn scarier. Man up, and start taking the reins for your future—with her or without her. You do have that child to worry about!
Dr. Gilda

Boyd's cheating friends had made him cynical. Their mantra was, "If you're not playing the game, then you're being played." A successful professional in his 40's, he had not had a serious relationship since college. In fact, now he rarely went out. He admitted that he immersed himself in the work he loved. He had only had two sexual partners in his life, both of who cheated on him. His cynical friends and his bad personal experiences ended his desire to try again. Socializing sharpens our skills to differentiate truth from game playing—a lesson Boyd was missing out on.

Boyd's game-player friends did not take love seriously, and he had mirrored their lead. I advised him to break his cycle immediately. The first step he needed to take was to exchange his former, jaundiced buddies for new ones with more positive dating outlooks.

In one of my Singles workshops, each person was asked to describe himself or herself as an animal. Allen wrote, "The animal I chose is a shark. Dating is a game. I am a bully when I have control over people. I prey on both the weak and the strong, especially when I have legitimate authority over them—whether I'm their boss or their lover. A shark represents a big scary bully. I always put myself first, and I admit that I'm extremely selfish. As long as I keep winning at this game of love, I'm fine with it."

Sharks have survived on earth for about 400 million years—so I had no doubt that Allen would continue his playing. But he later wrote on another Self-Assessment,

"Deep down inside, I am actually a very caring and sensitive person who doesn't like to show it. Most men don't like to share and show the soft, sensitive affections we have; I know I don't. I guess I am too concerned with how other people would react when I show these affections, especially when I am around my friends. A good example of this is when I am out with my friends playing ball in the park. When my fiancé approaches me, I try to act tough and avoid saying, 'I love you' around them, but I really do feel deeply for her. Even when I am on the phone with her and I have my friends around, I won't say it to her."

Arnold, another man in my workshop, agreed, "I know what you mean about having trouble showing your feelings. It can be especially difficult in front of friends."

While these guys insisted on keeping up their knightly game for the sake of "the guys," they also acknowledged that it was bringing them much stress to constantly have to wear their heavy and impenetrable armor!

Another workshop participant, Fred, said, "When it comes to women, I am a predator. I try to play it cool, and when I see a sign of weakness, I go for the kill. Like my animal, I like to hunt for new women. It feels good when I attract a new female without having to spend money or show off, but just by getting her to want me by being myself. As I said, if I see a sign of weakness, I am right in there, after that girl.

The key is not to get emotionally involved. Actually, I have recently cooled down with my women hunting. It started to get old to me, so now I'm waiting to meet my special partner. But until I find her, I do get a little hunting in every now and then."

Tom boldly responded to Allen and Fred. He said, "Go on, you players! You are right that it eventually gets old. I thought the same way you guys did when I was a little younger. I preyed on girls who were weak, I played a lot of games, I was extremely aggressive, and I hurt plenty of women. Now that I've become more mature, I am beginning to leave that behind, in favor of starting a family. I have cooled down and I'm hunting less."

Note that none of these guys said they were giving up the game of hunting entirely; they were just doing it "every now and then" or "less."

The game player's game plan is to play a game, without getting involved in long-term commitment.

<u>Gilda-Gram®</u>
If you sense your love's a game player,
switch to someone less gamey.

SIGN #10
Your Honey Craves Constant Attention from the Opposite Sex

Cheaters need endless stroking that no one person can ever fill. Their craving for attention reflects a need to boost their real feelings of inadequacy.

When lively Eliza met Richard, she was impressed by his quiet and secure-seeming shyness. Quickly, he confessed that he had fallen for her. The pair began a long-distance relationship. Eliza visited him often on weekends.

One day, she found photos and videos of this supposedly shy guy with some naked women. Friends had revealed earlier that Richard "had many female friends." Eliza didn't know how "friendly" he was with these so-called "friends." But she noticed he spent much time at nightclubs with "the boys," and he was always quick to erase his voice mail when she approached his phone. She was honest. She confronted him about what appeared to be a secret life he was having. Richard's excuse was that guys "always want more, and nothing is ever enough."

If Eliza had listened carefully, she would have acknowledged that this was Richard's true philosophy of love. He was a man who would forever crave more than what he already had with her. With great heartache, Eliza finally accepted the reality that she needed to move on.

People who feel good about themselves don't need continued and constant applause from the bleachers. They are satisfied with what they have with the partner they're with, and they show they are grateful for it by remaining committed and true to their one and only.

<u>Gilda-Gram®</u>
A partner with self-respect
knows how to respect you.

CONCLUSION

When You Find Your Honey is
NOT a "Honey"

You've read the SIGNS of a Cheater-to-Be. Some of them might be disturbing if you consider you've already been putting up with some raunchy stuff. But don't fret! Maybe from reading this you've learned that your love isn't such a love after all.

The most important thing is to know that life and love are all about learning. As I said earlier, even if your romance didn't work out as you had hoped,

Gilda-Gram®
Because he touched you, he taught you.

So let's now discover what you truly learned from the brute you've allowed to play in your life! Please note that I've deliberately worded this last sentence this way: "the brute you've *allowed* to play in your life."

It's time to accept that you permitted someone unworthy to stay in you life—until you finally got fed up enough to change the dance steps!

Self-Discovery

Instead of getting bummed about a cheater who stole your heart, list below what you LEARNED from the experience. This awareness is necessary so that you can apply it for a much more glorious future:

1)_____

2)_____

3)_____

Re-create your story of this love affair, but this time design it with a POSITIVE spin, ending exactly as you'd like it to be, even if it seems like a mushy fairy tale. It's YOUR fantasy story of YOUR life, so create its happy ending the way you want it to be.

The most important outcome of any relationship is not the relationship's longevity, but the amount that you have grown for having been in it. Your new insight and growth will arm you to attract someone far more worthy in your future. Of course, you'll make mistakes, but . . .

Gilda-Gram®
**For a relationship to have shelf life,
its foundation must be sturdy.**

Once in a new relationship, based on what you've just learned about yourself, it WILL begin with a sturdy foundation. You'll see to that!!

From now on, if you believe that something is not right, TRUST YOUR GUT that it's not right! Don't ever, ever, ever put your feelings under the mat to collect dust, and maybe be dealt with later. Your lover—and even you—will wipe your feet on it. As the mat becomes dirtier and more ingrained with soot, you'll forget what's underneath and how important your divine feelings really are. But your subconscious never forgets. It will be the cause of great suffering inside, which also prevents a relationship to thrive.

The SIGNS you see and feel are real. And you need to act on them as soon as you see them. No more pulling the wool over your eyes! If you keep telling yourself you deserve to enjoy only the very best, that's exactly what you'll get!

***

Benefit from
Dr. Gilda's personal Advice & Coaching
www.DrGilda.com

***

Dr. Gilda's Self-Worth Series
-- "I'm Worth Loving! Here's Why."
-- "Ask for What You Want—AND GET IT!
-- "How to Be a Worry-Free Woman"

Dr. Gilda's Relationship Series
--8 Steps to a Sizzling Marriage
--8 Tips to Understand the Opposite Sex
--10 Questions Single Women Should Never Ask
& 10 They Should
--10 Signs of a Cheater-to-Be

Dr. Gilda's Fidelity Series
--Why Your Cheater Keeps Cheating—And You're
Still There!
--How to Cope with the Cheater You Love—and
WIN!
--99 Prescriptions for Fidelity: *Your Rx for Trust*

ALSO
--Don't Bet on the Prince! *How to Have the Man You
Want by Betting on Yourself*
--Don't Lie on Your Back for a Guy Who Doesn't
Have Yours

***

Dr. Gilda Carle (Ph.D.) is an internationally known media personality and relationship expert. She has authored 15 books, including "Don't Bet on the Prince!" (a test question on "Jeopardy!"), "Teen Talk with Dr. Gilda," "He's Not All That!," "How to WIN When Your Mate Cheats" (winner of The London Book Festival literary award), "99 Prescriptions for Fidelity," and more. She also wrote the weekly "30-Second Therapist" column for the Today Show, and the "Ask Dr. Gilda" advice columnist for Match.com.

On TV, Dr. Gilda was the regular therapist for the Sally Jessy Raphael show, the "Love Doc" for MTV Online, and the TV host of "The Dr. Gilda Show" pilot for Twentieth Century Fox. In addition, she was the therapist in HBO's Emmy Award winner, "Telling Nicholas," featured on Oprah, where she guided a family to tell their 7-year-old that his mom died in the World Trade Center bombing.

In academia and the corporate sector, she has been a management consultant, Professor Emerita, motivational speaker, and product spokesperson.

Through her website, **www.DrGilda.com**, Dr. Gilda provides Advice and Coaching on Skype throughout the world.

As President of Country Cures, Inc., a non-profit 501(c)(3) educational charity organization, she is the "Country Music Doctor." The organization uniquely uses Country Music to provide relationship training for transitioning veterans and their families. If you, or someone you know, can benefit from this help, please see **www.CountryCures.org**.

————————

**Reach Dr. Gilda at
www.DrGilda.com
or
www.CountryCures.org**

www.ingramcontent.com/pod-product-compliance
Lightning Source LLC
Chambersburg PA
CBHW071645040426
42452CB00009B/1771